50 Premium Underwater Food Dishes

By: Kelly Johnson

Table of Contents

- Lobster Tail
- Caviar
- Oysters Rockefeller
- Grilled Sea Bass
- Sushi (Toro and Uni)
- Lobster Bisque
- Abalone with Truffle
- Seared Scallops
- Fish Tacos with Mango Salsa
- Clams Casino
- Tuna Tartare
- Lobster Newberg
- Salmon Roe
- Black Cod Miso
- Tempura Shrimp
- Grilled Swordfish
- Baked Oysters with Garlic Butter
- Salt-Crusted Whole Fish
- Sea Urchin (Uni)
- King Crab Legs
- Miso-Marinated Tuna
- Mussels in White Wine Sauce
- Lobster Roll
- Paella with Seafood
- Shrimp Cocktail
- Poke Bowl
- Grilled Octopus
- Smoked Salmon
- Squid Ink Risotto
- Fish Ceviche
- Seared Tuna with Wasabi
- Clam Chowder
- Blackened Red Snapper
- Grilled Mahi Mahi
- Tuna Sashimi
- Whole Roasted Lobster

- Oysters on the Half Shell
- Grilled Shrimp Skewers
- Fettuccine with Lobster
- Crab Cakes
- Salmon Fillet with Lemon Butter
- Seafood Ravioli
- Surf and Turf (Lobster and Steak)
- Seaweed Salad
- Lobster Mac and Cheese
- Baked Sea Bass with Herbs
- Scallop and Shrimp Skewers
- Bouillabaisse (French Seafood Stew)
- Blackened Mahi Mahi Tacos
- Fish and Chips

Lobster Tail

Ingredients:

- 2 lobster tails
- 2 tbsp melted butter
- 1 garlic clove, minced
- 1 tbsp lemon juice
- 1 tbsp fresh parsley, chopped
- Salt and pepper to taste

Instructions:

1. Preheat the oven to 425°F (220°C).
2. Using kitchen shears, cut the top shell of the lobster tails lengthwise, exposing the meat.
3. Carefully lift the meat out of the shell, but leave it attached at the base.
4. Place the lobster tails on a baking sheet, brushing them with melted butter, garlic, and lemon juice.
5. Season with salt and pepper, and sprinkle with parsley.
6. Bake for 12-15 minutes or until the lobster meat is opaque and cooked through.
7. Serve immediately with additional melted butter and lemon wedges.

Caviar

Ingredients:

- 2 oz caviar (of your choice: Beluga, Ossetra, or Sevruga)
- Blinis or crackers
- Crème fraîche
- Chopped chives (optional)
- Lemon wedges (optional)

Instructions:

1. Serve the caviar chilled, either on a plate or in a decorative dish.
2. Pair with blinis or crackers, and garnish with a dollop of crème fraîche.
3. Optionally, sprinkle with chopped chives or serve with lemon wedges.
4. Enjoy the caviar by itself or with the accompaniments.

Oysters Rockefeller

Ingredients:

- 12 fresh oysters, shucked
- 1/4 cup spinach, cooked and chopped
- 1/4 cup breadcrumbs
- 2 tbsp butter, melted
- 1 tbsp Pernod (optional)
- 2 tbsp grated Parmesan cheese
- Salt and pepper to taste

Instructions:

1. Preheat the oven to 450°F (230°C).
2. Place the shucked oysters on a baking sheet, ensuring they are stable.
3. In a bowl, mix the cooked spinach, breadcrumbs, melted butter, Pernod (optional), Parmesan cheese, and a pinch of salt and pepper.
4. Spoon the spinach mixture generously onto each oyster.
5. Bake for 10-12 minutes, until the topping is golden brown and the oysters are cooked through.
6. Serve immediately, garnished with extra Parmesan cheese and a squeeze of lemon.

Grilled Sea Bass

Ingredients:

- 2 sea bass fillets, skin-on
- 2 tbsp olive oil
- 1 tbsp lemon juice
- 1 tbsp fresh thyme or rosemary
- Salt and pepper to taste

Instructions:

1. Preheat the grill to medium-high heat.
2. Brush the sea bass fillets with olive oil, lemon juice, and season with salt, pepper, and fresh herbs.
3. Grill the fillets for 3-4 minutes on each side until the fish is cooked through and has grill marks.
4. Serve immediately with a drizzle of olive oil and fresh herbs.

Sushi (Toro and Uni)

Ingredients for Toro (Fatty Tuna):

- 4 oz toro (fatty tuna) sashimi, sliced thinly
- Soy sauce for dipping
- Wasabi and pickled ginger for garnish

Ingredients for Uni (Sea Urchin):

- 4 oz fresh uni (sea urchin roe)
- Sushi rice, prepared
- Nori (seaweed) sheets

Instructions:

1. For toro, slice the fatty tuna into thin pieces. Serve on a platter with soy sauce, wasabi, and pickled ginger.
2. For uni, place a small amount of sushi rice in the center of a nori sheet, then top with uni and roll the nori to create sushi.
3. Serve the sushi with additional wasabi and soy sauce on the side.

Lobster Bisque

Ingredients:

- 1 lb lobster meat, chopped
- 2 tbsp butter
- 1 onion, chopped
- 2 garlic cloves, minced
- 1/4 cup brandy or sherry
- 1 cup heavy cream
- 3 cups lobster stock or chicken broth
- 2 tbsp tomato paste
- 1 tsp paprika
- Salt and pepper to taste
- Fresh parsley for garnish

Instructions:

1. In a large pot, melt butter over medium heat and sauté the onion and garlic until softened.
2. Add the lobster meat and cook for 2-3 minutes.
3. Pour in the brandy or sherry and allow it to reduce for 2 minutes.
4. Add the tomato paste, paprika, and lobster stock. Simmer for 15-20 minutes.
5. Blend the soup with an immersion blender or regular blender until smooth.
6. Stir in the heavy cream and season with salt and pepper.
7. Serve garnished with fresh parsley.

Abalone with Truffle

Ingredients:

- 2 abalone, sliced
- 1 tbsp truffle oil
- 1 tbsp butter
- 1 garlic clove, minced
- 1 tbsp fresh parsley, chopped
- Salt and pepper to taste

Instructions:

1. Heat the butter and truffle oil in a pan over medium heat.
2. Add the garlic and sauté for 1 minute.
3. Add the sliced abalone and cook for 2-3 minutes per side until tender.
4. Season with salt and pepper, and garnish with fresh parsley.
5. Serve immediately, drizzled with additional truffle oil if desired.

Seared Scallops

Ingredients:

- 8 large scallops, patted dry
- 1 tbsp olive oil
- 1 tbsp butter
- Salt and pepper to taste
- Lemon wedges for serving

Instructions:

1. Heat olive oil in a skillet over medium-high heat.
2. Season the scallops with salt and pepper.
3. Sear the scallops for 2-3 minutes per side until golden brown and cooked through.
4. Add butter to the pan during the last minute of cooking for added flavor.
5. Serve with lemon wedges.

Fish Tacos with Mango Salsa

Ingredients for Mango Salsa:

- 1 ripe mango, diced
- 1/2 red onion, finely chopped
- 1 small jalapeño, minced
- 1 tbsp cilantro, chopped
- 1 tbsp lime juice
- Salt to taste

Ingredients for Fish Tacos:

- 2 fish fillets (such as tilapia or mahi-mahi), grilled or pan-fried
- 8 small corn tortillas
- 1/4 cup sour cream
- 1 tbsp lime juice
- 1 tbsp cilantro, chopped

Instructions:

1. In a bowl, mix the mango, red onion, jalapeño, cilantro, lime juice, and salt to make the salsa.
2. Grill or pan-fry the fish fillets, then flake the fish into bite-sized pieces.
3. In a small bowl, mix sour cream and lime juice to make the sauce.
4. Warm the tortillas and fill them with fish, mango salsa, and a drizzle of lime cream sauce.
5. Garnish with cilantro and serve immediately.

Clams Casino

Ingredients:

- 12 fresh clams, shucked
- 1/4 cup breadcrumbs
- 1/4 cup grated Parmesan cheese
- 2 tbsp butter, melted
- 1 tbsp garlic, minced
- 1 tbsp parsley, chopped
- 1 tbsp lemon juice
- Salt and pepper to taste

Instructions:

1. Preheat the oven to 450°F (230°C).
2. Place the clams on a baking sheet.
3. In a bowl, mix breadcrumbs, Parmesan cheese, butter, garlic, parsley, lemon juice, salt, and pepper.
4. Spoon the mixture onto each clam, pressing it gently to form a topping.
5. Bake for 8-10 minutes, until the topping is golden and the clams are cooked.
6. Serve immediately with lemon wedges.

Tuna Tartare

Ingredients:

- 8 oz sushi-grade tuna, finely diced
- 1 tbsp soy sauce
- 1 tsp sesame oil
- 1/2 tsp fresh lime juice
- 1/2 avocado, diced
- 1 tbsp green onions, chopped
- 1 tbsp sesame seeds
- Fresh cilantro for garnish
- Salt and pepper to taste

Instructions:

1. In a bowl, combine the diced tuna, soy sauce, sesame oil, and lime juice.
2. Gently fold in the diced avocado, green onions, and sesame seeds.
3. Season with salt and pepper to taste.
4. Serve in individual bowls or as a tartare stack, garnished with fresh cilantro.
5. Optionally, serve with crispy wonton chips or toasted baguette slices.

Lobster Newberg

Ingredients:

- 2 lobster tails, cooked and chopped
- 1/2 cup heavy cream
- 1/4 cup brandy (or cognac)
- 3 egg yolks
- 1 tbsp butter
- 1 tbsp fresh tarragon, chopped
- 1/4 cup grated Parmesan cheese
- Salt and pepper to taste
- 2 egg whites, whipped until stiff (optional, for garnish)

Instructions:

1. In a pan, melt butter over medium heat, then add brandy and cook for 1 minute.
2. Add the heavy cream and bring to a simmer.
3. Whisk the egg yolks into the sauce mixture, stirring continuously until it thickens.
4. Fold in the chopped lobster and tarragon.
5. Spoon the lobster mixture into ramekins or a serving dish.
6. Sprinkle with Parmesan cheese and bake in a preheated oven at 400°F (200°C) for 10 minutes until golden and bubbly.
7. Optionally, top with whipped egg whites for extra fluffiness and garnish with fresh herbs.

Salmon Roe

Ingredients:

- 4 oz fresh salmon roe (ikura)
- 2 tbsp soy sauce
- 1 tsp rice vinegar
- 1 tsp mirin
- 1 tsp sesame oil
- Small cucumber, julienned (for garnish)
- 1 tbsp chopped chives (optional)

Instructions:

1. Gently rinse the salmon roe under cold water and drain.
2. Mix soy sauce, rice vinegar, mirin, and sesame oil to make a marinade.
3. Carefully toss the roe in the marinade and let it sit for about 15-20 minutes.
4. Serve the roe in small bowls or on sushi rice, garnished with julienned cucumber and chives.

Black Cod Miso

Ingredients:

- 4 black cod fillets (6 oz each)
- 1/4 cup white miso paste
- 2 tbsp mirin
- 2 tbsp sake
- 2 tbsp sugar
- 1 tbsp soy sauce
- 1 tbsp grated ginger

Instructions:

1. In a bowl, mix the miso paste, mirin, sake, sugar, soy sauce, and grated ginger to make the marinade.
2. Place the cod fillets in a shallow dish and pour the marinade over them.
3. Cover and refrigerate for at least 2 hours or overnight.
4. Preheat the oven to 400°F (200°C).
5. Place the fillets on a baking sheet lined with parchment paper and bake for 10-12 minutes, until the fish is cooked through and caramelized on top.
6. Serve with steamed rice and vegetables.

Tempura Shrimp

Ingredients:

- 12 large shrimp, peeled and deveined
- 1/2 cup rice flour
- 1/2 cup all-purpose flour
- 1/2 tsp baking powder
- 1/2 cup ice-cold sparkling water
- Salt to taste
- Vegetable oil for frying

Instructions:

1. Heat vegetable oil in a deep fryer or large pot to 350°F (175°C).
2. In a bowl, mix rice flour, all-purpose flour, and baking powder.
3. Gradually add the sparkling water, stirring until just combined (do not overmix).
4. Dip the shrimp into the batter, ensuring they are evenly coated.
5. Fry the shrimp in batches for 2-3 minutes until golden and crispy.
6. Drain on paper towels and season with salt.
7. Serve with dipping sauce (soy sauce or tempura sauce) and garnish with lemon wedges.

Grilled Swordfish

Ingredients:

- 2 swordfish steaks (6 oz each)
- 1 tbsp olive oil
- 1 tbsp lemon juice
- 1 tsp garlic powder
- Salt and pepper to taste

Instructions:

1. Preheat the grill to medium-high heat.
2. Brush the swordfish steaks with olive oil and lemon juice.
3. Season with garlic powder, salt, and pepper.
4. Grill the steaks for 4-5 minutes per side, or until the fish is cooked through and slightly charred.
5. Serve with extra lemon wedges and fresh herbs.

Baked Oysters with Garlic Butter

Ingredients:

- 12 fresh oysters, shucked
- 1/4 cup butter, melted
- 2 garlic cloves, minced
- 1 tbsp parsley, chopped
- 1 tbsp grated Parmesan cheese
- 1 tbsp lemon juice
- Salt and pepper to taste

Instructions:

1. Preheat the oven to 400°F (200°C).
2. In a bowl, combine melted butter, garlic, parsley, Parmesan, lemon juice, salt, and pepper.
3. Spoon the garlic butter mixture onto each oyster.
4. Arrange the oysters on a baking sheet and bake for 10-12 minutes, until golden and bubbly.
5. Serve immediately with lemon wedges.

Salt-Crusted Whole Fish

Ingredients:

- 1 whole fish (such as snapper or sea bass), gutted and cleaned
- 3 lbs kosher salt
- 1 egg white
- 1/4 cup fresh herbs (thyme, rosemary, parsley)
- Lemon slices for garnish

Instructions:

1. Preheat the oven to 400°F (200°C).
2. In a bowl, mix kosher salt with egg whites to create a dough-like consistency.
3. Stuff the fish with fresh herbs and place it on a baking sheet.
4. Cover the fish entirely with the salt mixture, pressing it gently around the fish.
5. Bake for 20-25 minutes, until the salt crust is golden and firm.
6. Break the salt crust open and serve the fish with lemon slices.

Sea Urchin (Uni)

Ingredients:

- Fresh uni (sea urchin roe)
- Sushi rice, prepared
- Nori (seaweed) sheets (optional)
- Soy sauce for dipping
- Wasabi (optional)

Instructions:

1. Carefully remove the uni from its shell.
2. Serve the uni on a small bed of sushi rice, or wrapped in a small piece of nori.
3. Drizzle with soy sauce and add wasabi if desired.
4. Enjoy immediately for the best freshness.

King Crab Legs

Ingredients:

- 2-3 king crab legs (or more, depending on serving size)
- 4 tbsp butter, melted
- 1 garlic clove, minced
- 1 tbsp lemon juice
- Fresh parsley, chopped

Instructions:

1. Preheat the oven to 375°F (190°C).
2. Place the king crab legs on a baking sheet and cover them with aluminum foil.
3. Bake for 10-12 minutes until heated through.
4. In a small bowl, mix the melted butter, garlic, and lemon juice.
5. Serve the crab legs with the garlic butter sauce and garnish with fresh parsley.

Miso-Marinated Tuna

Ingredients:

- 2 tuna steaks (6 oz each)
- 1/4 cup white miso paste
- 2 tbsp soy sauce
- 1 tbsp mirin
- 1 tbsp rice vinegar
- 1 tsp sesame oil
- 1 tsp grated ginger
- 1 tbsp green onions, chopped (for garnish)
- Sesame seeds (optional)

Instructions:

1. In a bowl, combine miso paste, soy sauce, mirin, rice vinegar, sesame oil, and grated ginger.
2. Coat the tuna steaks with the marinade and let them marinate in the refrigerator for at least 30 minutes to 1 hour.
3. Heat a grill or grill pan over medium-high heat.
4. Grill the tuna for 2-3 minutes per side for a medium-rare finish, or longer depending on your desired level of doneness.
5. Garnish with chopped green onions and sesame seeds before serving.

Mussels in White Wine Sauce

Ingredients:

- 2 lbs fresh mussels, cleaned and debearded
- 1 tbsp olive oil
- 3 garlic cloves, minced
- 1/2 cup dry white wine
- 1/2 cup heavy cream
- 1/4 cup fresh parsley, chopped
- 1 tbsp lemon juice
- Salt and pepper to taste

Instructions:

1. In a large pot, heat olive oil over medium heat. Add minced garlic and sauté for 1 minute until fragrant.
2. Pour in the white wine and bring to a simmer.
3. Add the mussels to the pot and cover with a lid. Let them steam for 5-7 minutes, or until the mussels have opened.
4. Stir in the heavy cream, lemon juice, parsley, salt, and pepper.
5. Cook for an additional 1-2 minutes until the sauce has thickened slightly.
6. Serve the mussels in a bowl, spooning the sauce over the top.

Lobster Roll

Ingredients:

- 2 lobster tails (cooked and chopped)
- 1/4 cup mayonnaise
- 1 tbsp fresh lemon juice
- 1 tsp Dijon mustard
- 1 tbsp fresh chives, chopped
- 4 top-split buns (preferably New England-style)
- 2 tbsp butter
- Salt and pepper to taste

Instructions:

1. In a bowl, combine mayonnaise, lemon juice, Dijon mustard, chives, salt, and pepper.
2. Gently fold the chopped lobster into the mayo mixture.
3. Heat butter in a skillet over medium heat and toast the buns until golden.
4. Fill the toasted buns with the lobster mixture and serve immediately.

Paella with Seafood

Ingredients:

- 1 tbsp olive oil
- 1 onion, chopped
- 2 garlic cloves, minced
- 1 bell pepper, chopped
- 1 1/2 cups Arborio rice (or paella rice)
- 1/2 tsp saffron threads (soaked in 1/4 cup warm water)
- 1 1/2 cups chicken broth
- 1 1/2 cups seafood broth
- 1 cup dry white wine
- 1 lb mixed seafood (shrimp, mussels, clams, squid, etc.)
- 1/2 cup frozen peas
- Salt and pepper to taste
- Fresh parsley and lemon wedges for garnish

Instructions:

1. In a large pan or paella pan, heat olive oil over medium heat. Add onion, garlic, and bell pepper and sauté for 5 minutes.
2. Add the rice and cook for another 2-3 minutes, stirring occasionally.
3. Pour in the wine and cook until it has evaporated.
4. Add the saffron with its soaking water, chicken broth, seafood broth, and salt. Bring to a simmer, then reduce heat to low.
5. Arrange the seafood over the rice and cook for 10-15 minutes until the seafood is cooked through and the rice has absorbed the liquid.
6. Stir in the peas, cook for an additional 5 minutes.
7. Garnish with fresh parsley and lemon wedges.

Shrimp Cocktail

Ingredients:

- 1 lb large shrimp, peeled and deveined
- 1/4 cup lemon juice
- 1 bay leaf
- 1 tsp Old Bay seasoning
- 1/2 tsp salt
- 1 cup cocktail sauce (store-bought or homemade)

Instructions:

1. In a pot, combine water, lemon juice, bay leaf, Old Bay seasoning, and salt. Bring to a boil.
2. Add the shrimp and cook for 2-3 minutes, or until they turn pink and opaque.
3. Remove the shrimp and transfer them to an ice bath to cool.
4. Serve the chilled shrimp with cocktail sauce for dipping.

Poke Bowl

Ingredients:

- 1 lb sushi-grade tuna or salmon, diced
- 2 tbsp soy sauce
- 1 tbsp sesame oil
- 1 tbsp rice vinegar
- 1 tsp honey or sugar
- 1 avocado, sliced
- 1/4 cup cucumber, thinly sliced
- 1/4 cup edamame, cooked
- 1/4 cup shredded carrots
- 1/2 cup cooked rice (preferably sushi rice)
- 1 tbsp sesame seeds
- 1 tsp chili flakes (optional)

Instructions:

1. In a bowl, combine the diced tuna or salmon with soy sauce, sesame oil, rice vinegar, and honey or sugar. Toss to coat and let marinate for 10-15 minutes.
2. Assemble the poke bowl by placing a scoop of rice at the bottom of a bowl.
3. Arrange the marinated fish, avocado, cucumber, edamame, and carrots on top of the rice.
4. Garnish with sesame seeds, chili flakes, and extra soy sauce if desired.

Grilled Octopus

Ingredients:

- 1 lb octopus tentacles, cleaned
- 1/4 cup olive oil
- 2 garlic cloves, minced
- 1 tbsp lemon juice
- 1 tsp smoked paprika
- Salt and pepper to taste
- Fresh parsley for garnish

Instructions:

1. Boil the octopus in a large pot of water for 45-60 minutes, or until tender. Drain and let cool.
2. Heat olive oil in a small pan over medium heat. Add garlic and sauté for 1 minute.
3. Brush the octopus with the garlic oil mixture, then season with smoked paprika, salt, and pepper.
4. Preheat a grill or grill pan over medium-high heat. Grill the octopus for 3-4 minutes per side, or until charred and crispy.
5. Garnish with fresh parsley and serve with lemon wedges.

Smoked Salmon

Ingredients:

- 1 lb fresh salmon fillet
- 1/4 cup brown sugar
- 1/4 cup kosher salt
- 1 tbsp cracked black pepper
- 1 tbsp dill, chopped
- 1 tbsp lemon zest
- 1 tsp mustard seeds (optional)

Instructions:

1. In a bowl, mix brown sugar, kosher salt, black pepper, dill, lemon zest, and mustard seeds.
2. Rub the mixture evenly over the salmon fillet, cover with plastic wrap, and refrigerate for 12-24 hours.
3. After curing, rinse the salmon gently under cold water to remove excess brine.
4. Smoke the salmon on a smoker for 2-3 hours at 180°F (82°C) or until fully cooked and smoky.
5. Slice thinly and serve with bagels, cream cheese, and capers.

Squid Ink Risotto

Ingredients:

- 1 cup Arborio rice
- 1/4 cup white wine
- 4 cups seafood broth
- 1 tbsp olive oil
- 2 garlic cloves, minced
- 1/4 cup shallots, finely chopped
- 1/4 cup squid ink
- 1/2 lb squid, cleaned and sliced
- 1 tbsp butter
- Salt and pepper to taste
- Fresh parsley for garnish

Instructions:

1. In a pan, heat olive oil over medium heat and sauté garlic and shallots for 2-3 minutes.
2. Add the Arborio rice and stir to coat with oil for 1-2 minutes.
3. Pour in the white wine and cook until it has absorbed.
4. Gradually add the seafood broth, one ladle at a time, stirring constantly, until the rice is creamy and cooked (about 18-20 minutes).
5. Stir in the squid ink, cooked squid, butter, salt, and pepper.
6. Garnish with fresh parsley and serve immediately.

Fish Ceviche

Ingredients:

- 1 lb fresh white fish (such as tilapia or halibut), diced
- 1/2 cup fresh lime juice
- 1/2 cup fresh lemon juice
- 1 small red onion, finely chopped
- 1/2 cup diced cucumber
- 1/2 cup diced tomato
- 1/4 cup cilantro, chopped
- 1 small chili pepper, finely chopped (optional)
- Salt and pepper to taste
- Tortilla chips (for serving)

Instructions:

1. In a bowl, combine the diced fish with lime and lemon juice.
2. Cover and refrigerate for 2-4 hours, allowing the fish to "cook" in the citrus juice.
3. Once the fish has turned opaque, add the red onion, cucumber, tomato, cilantro, chili pepper, salt, and pepper.
4. Stir to combine and serve with tortilla chips.

Seared Tuna with Wasabi

Ingredients:

- 2 tuna steaks (6 oz each)
- 1 tbsp sesame oil
- 2 tbsp soy sauce
- 1 tsp wasabi paste
- 1 tsp honey
- 1 tbsp sesame seeds (optional)
- Salt and pepper to taste

Instructions:

1. In a small bowl, mix soy sauce, wasabi paste, honey, and a pinch of salt and pepper.
2. Heat sesame oil in a skillet over high heat.
3. Sear the tuna steaks for 1-2 minutes on each side, until the outside is crispy but the inside remains rare.
4. Brush the tuna steaks with the wasabi sauce and sprinkle with sesame seeds (if using).
5. Serve immediately with a side of rice or vegetables.

Clam Chowder

Ingredients:

- 1 lb fresh clams, scrubbed and shucked
- 4 slices bacon, chopped
- 1 small onion, chopped
- 2 celery stalks, chopped
- 1 large potato, peeled and diced
- 3 cups clam juice
- 1 cup heavy cream
- 1/2 cup milk
- 1 tsp thyme
- Salt and pepper to taste
- Fresh parsley for garnish

Instructions:

1. In a large pot, cook bacon over medium heat until crispy. Remove bacon and set aside.
2. Add the onion and celery to the bacon fat and cook until softened, about 5 minutes.
3. Add the diced potato, clam juice, and thyme. Bring to a boil, then simmer until the potatoes are tender (about 15 minutes).
4. Stir in the heavy cream and milk, and bring the chowder to a simmer again.
5. Add the clams and cook until they are just heated through.
6. Season with salt and pepper to taste, and garnish with the cooked bacon and fresh parsley.

Blackened Red Snapper

Ingredients:

- 2 red snapper fillets
- 2 tbsp paprika
- 1 tbsp cayenne pepper
- 1 tbsp garlic powder
- 1 tbsp onion powder
- 1 tsp thyme
- 1 tsp oregano
- 1/2 tsp salt
- 1/2 tsp black pepper
- 2 tbsp butter
- 1 tbsp olive oil

Instructions:

1. In a small bowl, combine the paprika, cayenne, garlic powder, onion powder, thyme, oregano, salt, and pepper.
2. Coat the red snapper fillets evenly with the spice mixture.
3. Heat butter and olive oil in a skillet over medium-high heat.
4. Add the fillets to the pan and cook for 4-5 minutes on each side until the fish is cooked through and crispy on the outside.
5. Serve with a squeeze of fresh lemon.

Grilled Mahi Mahi

Ingredients:

- 2 mahi mahi fillets
- 2 tbsp olive oil
- 1 tbsp lime juice
- 1 tsp garlic powder
- 1 tsp paprika
- Salt and pepper to taste

Instructions:

1. Preheat the grill to medium-high heat.
2. In a small bowl, mix olive oil, lime juice, garlic powder, paprika, salt, and pepper.
3. Brush the mahi mahi fillets with the marinade.
4. Grill the fillets for 4-5 minutes on each side until the fish is cooked through and has grill marks.
5. Serve with extra lime wedges and your favorite side dish.

Tuna Sashimi

Ingredients:

- 1 lb sushi-grade tuna
- Soy sauce (for dipping)
- Wasabi and pickled ginger (for serving)

Instructions:

1. Slice the tuna into thin slices (about 1/4 inch thick).
2. Arrange the slices on a plate, fanning them out.
3. Serve with soy sauce, wasabi, and pickled ginger.

Whole Roasted Lobster

Ingredients:

- 2 live lobsters
- 4 tbsp butter, melted
- 2 garlic cloves, minced
- 1 tbsp fresh parsley, chopped
- Lemon wedges (for serving)

Instructions:

1. Preheat your oven to 375°F (190°C).
2. Bring a large pot of salted water to a boil. Add the lobsters and cook for 6-8 minutes until they turn bright red.
3. Remove the lobsters and let them cool slightly.
4. Split the lobsters in half and remove the meat from the shells.
5. Place the lobster halves on a baking sheet.
6. In a small bowl, combine melted butter, garlic, and parsley. Brush the mixture over the lobster meat.
7. Roast the lobsters in the oven for 10-12 minutes.
8. Serve with lemon wedges.

Oysters on the Half Shell

Ingredients:

- 12 fresh oysters
- Lemon wedges
- Mignonette sauce (optional)

Instructions:

1. Using an oyster knife, carefully shuck the oysters and place them on a platter.
2. Serve with lemon wedges and mignonette sauce (if desired).

Grilled Shrimp Skewers

Ingredients:

- 1 lb large shrimp, peeled and deveined
- 2 tbsp olive oil
- 1 tbsp lemon juice
- 2 garlic cloves, minced
- 1 tsp paprika
- Salt and pepper to taste
- Wooden or metal skewers

Instructions:

1. Preheat the grill to medium-high heat.
2. In a bowl, toss the shrimp with olive oil, lemon juice, garlic, paprika, salt, and pepper.
3. Thread the shrimp onto skewers.
4. Grill the shrimp for 2-3 minutes on each side until they are pink and opaque.
5. Serve with additional lemon wedges.

Fettuccine with Lobster

Ingredients:

- 2 lobster tails
- 8 oz fettuccine pasta
- 2 tbsp butter
- 2 garlic cloves, minced
- 1/2 cup heavy cream
- 1/2 cup white wine
- 1/4 cup Parmesan cheese, grated
- Salt and pepper to taste
- Fresh parsley for garnish

Instructions:

1. Cook the fettuccine pasta according to package directions.
2. In a separate pan, melt butter over medium heat. Add garlic and sauté for 1-2 minutes.
3. Add the lobster tails (shelled and chopped) to the pan and cook for 2-3 minutes.
4. Add white wine and simmer until the lobster is cooked through.
5. Stir in the heavy cream, Parmesan, salt, and pepper, cooking until the sauce thickens.
6. Toss the cooked pasta with the lobster sauce and garnish with parsley.

Crab Cakes

Ingredients:

- 1 lb crab meat (preferably lump or jumbo lump)
- 1/4 cup breadcrumbs
- 1/4 cup mayonnaise
- 1 egg
- 1 tbsp Dijon mustard
- 1 tbsp fresh parsley, chopped
- 1 tsp Old Bay seasoning
- 1 tsp Worcestershire sauce
- 1 tbsp lemon juice
- Salt and pepper to taste
- Vegetable oil for frying

Instructions:

1. In a bowl, combine the crab meat, breadcrumbs, mayonnaise, egg, mustard, parsley, Old Bay seasoning, Worcestershire sauce, lemon juice, salt, and pepper.
2. Gently mix until just combined. Form the mixture into patties (about 4-6, depending on your preferred size).
3. Heat vegetable oil in a skillet over medium-high heat.
4. Cook the crab cakes for 3-4 minutes on each side until golden brown and crispy.
5. Serve with lemon wedges and your favorite sauce, like tartar sauce or aioli.

Salmon Fillet with Lemon Butter

Ingredients:

- 2 salmon fillets
- 2 tbsp butter
- 1 tbsp lemon juice
- 1 garlic clove, minced
- 1 tsp fresh dill, chopped
- Salt and pepper to taste
- Lemon wedges for serving

Instructions:

1. Preheat the oven to 375°F (190°C).
2. Season the salmon fillets with salt and pepper.
3. Heat a skillet over medium-high heat and melt the butter.
4. Add the garlic to the pan and cook for 1 minute until fragrant.
5. Place the salmon fillets in the skillet, skin-side down. Cook for 4-5 minutes until the skin is crispy.
6. Transfer the pan to the oven and bake for 8-10 minutes until the salmon is cooked through.
7. Remove from the oven and drizzle with lemon juice, fresh dill, and additional melted butter.
8. Serve with lemon wedges.

Seafood Ravioli

Ingredients:

- 1 package of fresh or frozen seafood ravioli (or homemade if preferred)
- 1 tbsp olive oil
- 1/2 cup heavy cream
- 1/4 cup grated Parmesan cheese
- 1 garlic clove, minced
- 1/4 tsp red pepper flakes (optional)
- Salt and pepper to taste
- Fresh parsley for garnish

Instructions:

1. Cook the ravioli according to package instructions.
2. In a pan, heat olive oil over medium heat and sauté the garlic for 1 minute.
3. Add the heavy cream to the pan and simmer for 2-3 minutes until it thickens slightly.
4. Stir in the Parmesan cheese, red pepper flakes (if using), salt, and pepper.
5. Add the cooked ravioli to the sauce and toss to coat.
6. Serve immediately, garnished with fresh parsley.

Surf and Turf (Lobster and Steak)

Ingredients:

- 2 lobster tails
- 2 ribeye or filet mignon steaks
- 2 tbsp butter
- 1 garlic clove, minced
- 1 tbsp fresh thyme
- 1 tbsp fresh rosemary
- Salt and pepper to taste
- Olive oil for searing

Instructions:

1. Preheat your oven to 375°F (190°C).
2. Season the steaks with salt, pepper, and fresh thyme and rosemary.
3. Heat olive oil in a skillet over high heat. Sear the steaks for 3-4 minutes on each side, then transfer to the oven to finish cooking to your desired doneness (about 5-7 minutes for medium-rare).
4. While the steaks are cooking, prepare the lobster tails by cutting the shells down the center and removing the meat.
5. In a separate skillet, melt butter over medium heat. Add garlic and lobster meat, cooking for 3-4 minutes until the lobster is cooked through.
6. Serve the steaks with the lobster on top, garnished with fresh herbs and a drizzle of garlic butter.

Seaweed Salad

Ingredients:

- 1 cup dried wakame seaweed
- 1/4 cup rice vinegar
- 1 tbsp soy sauce
- 1 tbsp sesame oil
- 1 tbsp sugar
- 1/2 tsp salt
- 1 tbsp sesame seeds
- 1/2 cucumber, thinly sliced
- 1 small carrot, julienned (optional)

Instructions:

1. Rehydrate the wakame seaweed by soaking it in warm water for about 10 minutes. Drain and pat dry.
2. In a bowl, whisk together rice vinegar, soy sauce, sesame oil, sugar, and salt.
3. Add the rehydrated seaweed, cucumber slices, and julienned carrot (if using) to the dressing and toss to combine.
4. Sprinkle sesame seeds over the salad and serve chilled.

Lobster Mac and Cheese

Ingredients:

- 1 lb cooked lobster meat, chopped
- 8 oz elbow macaroni (or pasta of your choice)
- 2 tbsp butter
- 1 small onion, chopped
- 2 garlic cloves, minced
- 2 tbsp flour
- 2 cups whole milk
- 2 cups shredded cheddar cheese
- 1/2 cup grated Parmesan cheese
- Salt and pepper to taste
- Fresh parsley for garnish

Instructions:

1. Cook the pasta according to package instructions. Drain and set aside.
2. In a large pan, melt butter over medium heat. Add the chopped onion and garlic and sauté for 2-3 minutes until softened.
3. Sprinkle in the flour and whisk to create a roux. Cook for 1-2 minutes.
4. Gradually pour in the milk, whisking constantly to prevent lumps. Simmer for 3-4 minutes until the sauce thickens.
5. Stir in the cheddar and Parmesan cheese, continuing to whisk until the cheese melts and the sauce is smooth.
6. Add the cooked lobster meat and pasta to the sauce, tossing to coat.
7. Season with salt and pepper to taste, then garnish with fresh parsley before serving.

Baked Sea Bass with Herbs

Ingredients:

- 2 sea bass fillets
- 2 tbsp olive oil
- 2 garlic cloves, minced
- 1 tbsp fresh parsley, chopped
- 1 tbsp fresh thyme
- 1 lemon, sliced
- Salt and pepper to taste

Instructions:

1. Preheat your oven to 375°F (190°C).
2. Place the sea bass fillets on a baking sheet lined with parchment paper.
3. Drizzle the fillets with olive oil and season with salt, pepper, garlic, parsley, and thyme.
4. Lay lemon slices on top of the fillets.
5. Bake for 12-15 minutes, or until the fish is cooked through and flakes easily with a fork.
6. Serve with extra lemon wedges for garnish.

Scallop and Shrimp Skewers

Ingredients:

- 6 large shrimp, peeled and deveined
- 6 scallops
- 1 tbsp olive oil
- 1 tbsp lemon juice
- 2 garlic cloves, minced
- 1 tsp paprika
- Salt and pepper to taste
- Skewers (wooden or metal)

Instructions:

1. Preheat your grill or grill pan to medium-high heat.
2. In a bowl, combine olive oil, lemon juice, garlic, paprika, salt, and pepper.
3. Thread the shrimp and scallops alternately onto the skewers.
4. Brush the skewers with the marinade and let them sit for 10 minutes to soak in the flavors.
5. Grill the skewers for 2-3 minutes per side, until the seafood is cooked through and opaque.
6. Serve with extra lemon wedges and fresh herbs if desired.

Bouillabaisse (French Seafood Stew)

Ingredients:

- 1 lb white fish fillets (such as cod or snapper), cut into chunks
- 1/2 lb shrimp, peeled and deveined
- 1/2 lb mussels, scrubbed
- 1/2 lb clams, scrubbed
- 2 tbsp olive oil
- 1 onion, chopped
- 2 garlic cloves, minced
- 1 leek, sliced
- 1 carrot, sliced
- 2 tomatoes, diced
- 1 tbsp tomato paste
- 4 cups fish stock
- 1/2 cup dry white wine
- 1 tsp dried thyme
- 1 tsp saffron threads
- Salt and pepper to taste
- Fresh parsley, chopped (for garnish)

Instructions:

1. Heat olive oil in a large pot over medium heat. Add the onion, garlic, leek, and carrot, and sauté until softened, about 5 minutes.
2. Stir in the diced tomatoes and tomato paste, and cook for another 3 minutes.
3. Add the fish stock, white wine, thyme, saffron, salt, and pepper. Bring to a boil, then reduce the heat and simmer for 10 minutes.
4. Add the white fish, shrimp, mussels, and clams to the pot. Cook for an additional 10-12 minutes, or until the seafood is cooked through and the mussels and clams have opened.
5. Discard any unopened shells.
6. Serve the bouillabaisse hot, garnished with fresh parsley and crusty bread.

Blackened Mahi Mahi Tacos

Ingredients:

- 2 mahi mahi fillets
- 1 tbsp olive oil
- 1 tbsp paprika
- 1 tsp cayenne pepper
- 1 tsp garlic powder
- 1 tsp onion powder
- 1 tsp dried oregano
- Salt and pepper to taste
- 4 small tortillas
- 1 cup shredded cabbage
- 1/2 cup sour cream
- 1 tbsp lime juice
- Fresh cilantro for garnish

Instructions:

1. Preheat a skillet or grill pan over medium-high heat.
2. In a small bowl, mix the paprika, cayenne, garlic powder, onion powder, oregano, salt, and pepper.
3. Rub the spice mixture all over the mahi mahi fillets.
4. Drizzle olive oil into the skillet and cook the fish for 4-5 minutes per side, until the fish is blackened and cooked through.
5. While the fish cooks, combine the sour cream and lime juice in a small bowl.
6. Warm the tortillas in a dry pan or microwave.
7. To assemble the tacos, place a few pieces of mahi mahi on each tortilla, top with shredded cabbage, a drizzle of lime sour cream, and fresh cilantro.
8. Serve immediately with extra lime wedges.

Fish and Chips

Ingredients:

- 4 white fish fillets (cod, haddock, or pollock)
- 1 1/2 cups all-purpose flour, divided
- 1 tsp baking powder
- 1 tsp salt
- 1 cup cold sparkling water
- Vegetable oil for frying
- 4 large potatoes, peeled and cut into fries
- Salt to taste
- Tartar sauce for serving

Instructions:

1. Preheat oil in a deep fryer or large pot to 375°F (190°C).
2. In a bowl, combine 1 cup of flour, baking powder, and salt. Slowly whisk in the sparkling water until the batter is smooth and thick.
3. Dredge the fish fillets in the remaining flour, then dip them in the batter to coat.
4. Fry the fish fillets in the hot oil for 4-5 minutes until golden and crispy. Remove and drain on paper towels.
5. Meanwhile, fry the potato fries for 3-4 minutes until golden brown and crispy. Drain on paper towels and sprinkle with salt.
6. Serve the fish and chips hot with tartar sauce and lemon wedges.

www.ingramcontent.com/pod-product-compliance
Lightning Source LLC
LaVergne TN
LVHW081501060526
838201LV00056BA/2872